Journey to Purpose

Journey
To Purpose

31 Days of Faith Declarations

Deborah Robinson

Robinson Omnimedia Studios & Publishing

Little Rock . Nashville . Seattle . Phoenix

Published in the United States by

Robinson Omnimedia Publishing & Studios

Little Rock . Nashville . Seattle . Phoenix

www.RobinsonOmnimedia.com

ISBN: 1453782044

EAN-13 is 9781453782040

Journey to Purpose: 31 Days of Faith Declarations
First Edition - July 2000
Second Internet Edition - March 2002
Third Edition - October 2004
Fourth Edition - August 2010

[written by] Deborah Robinson
[edited by] Marie Trotter. –1st ed.

PUBLISHER'S NOTE

Faith Declarations are interpreted, translated and written by
Deborah Robinson using diverse study guides and various
Holy Bible translations.

To my mother, Essie Bradford,
for starting me on my Journey to Purpose.

JourneytoPurpose.com

CONTENTS

Faith is the assurance of things we hope for
and the evidence of things we cannot see.

Hebrews 11:1

ABOUT THE AUTHOR

*D*EBORAH ROBINSON IS an award-winning journalist, author and television personality. Her ventures include Deborah, Inc., The Deborah Interviews Show, Robinson Omnimedia Publishing & Studios and Green Orchards. Her life's passion is to reveal and communicate truth through her work in the media.

I pray that God grants you a spirit of wisdom, intimate insight and deep revelation into the mysteries and secrets of Him. I pray the eyes of your heart be flooded with light so that you may know and understand the hope to which He has called you. Godspeed in your Journey to Purpose!

Love Deborah

INTRODUCTION

*T*hese Declarations of Faith were written out of my desire to develop, in my own life, the mountain-moving faith Jesus speaks of in Matthew 17:20. He says if we have faith as a grain of mustard seed, we can say to our mountains, "*Move from here to there, and it will move. Nothing will be impossible for you.*" My desire is to develop the kind of faith that moves mountains. I no longer want strength to climb my mountains. I want to say, in faith, never wavering and without doubting, "*Mountain...Be Thou Removed*" and I want to watch it be tossed into the sea. Whatever your mountain may be, as you declare these Declarations of Faith, don't believe in the words alone, but put your faith in the God whose Words will not return unto Him until they have accomplished His purpose.

Declaring and confessing God's Word over our lives is essential to maintaining faith in His promises. I have long recognized the benefits of confessing the promises of God in my life. While taping for my daily television Faith Declarations segments, I experienced the awesome power of these confessions. As my photographer prepared for the shooting, I was reviewing the Faith Declarations. As I read one of the scriptures, I began to sing it. As I sang it, I became overwhelmed. The scripture began to take root in my spirit and come alive in my life. I don't know how long I sang and wept, but my camera operator cut off the equipment. I found him in the control room asleep.

This book chronicles my personal journey to purpose. Before ever considering writing it, I lived it. The corresponding scriptures are Words that strengthened my faith while facing unbelief, doubt and other hindrances. I pray these Faith Declarations will help you faithfully walk with God, no matter how crooked the path may seem. I pray you realize, as I have, that there is no purpose, no destiny, no vision, and no reason for existing without God. It is He that leads us on this journey to purpose.

Without a fresh Word from God daily, I have no direction. Faith Declarations are my daily manna. They are my food on a journey paved with obstacles and distractions. I have lived each Faith Declaration over and over with new revelation with each new experience. Each day represents a season in my journey to purpose. There are seasons of praying, trusting, seeking, resisting, obeying, working, waiting, believing, praising and even seasons of fear, doubt and unbelief. His Word breathes life into me again and again as I face them all, especially the latter three. Every time I encounter a "*doubting Thomas*," someone who can't understand my walk of faith and only believes what he sees, I turn to I Corinthians 2:9 and declare *"eyes have not seen, ears have not heard, neither has it entered into the heart of man the magnitude of what God has prepared for me."* I realize others may not be able to see the vision God has given me for my life - and that's OK. The Word said it would be this way. I am then comforted by verse 10 as I proclaim *"God has unveiled and revealed His plans for my life to me by and through His Spirit, Which searches diligently, exploring and examining everything, even the deep things of God and the things hidden and beyond man's scrutiny."*

Having received my share of scrutiny, I know well the doubt it can cast in your mind; unbelief that causes you to question the Words of God concerning you. But as I consider what else I can do with my life, with all the talent God has blessed me with, I can think of nothing. Without God, I am nothing and I have nothing. My journey to purpose is life or death. There is no other reason for my existence. This purpose inside of me... lives.

Through Faith Declarations, I continue on the journey, recycling lesson after lesson, moving from season to season and glory to glory. Use this book to journal your personal journey to purpose or to develop your own faith declarations from scriptures that deal with your life experiences. When you're in each day's season, memorize and meditate on the words of that Declaration. Say them out loud. Hear them. Faith comes by hearing. Allow them to resonate in your spirit. The Word of God will come alive in your life. He promises!

Without faith it is impossible to please God.

Hebrews 11:6

TRUST IN GOD

DECLARE - I will trust in God with all my heart and lean not unto my own understanding or intelligence. In all my ways, I will acknowledge Him. He will make my path plain, straight and visible. I will trust in God with all my heart. He will direct my path.

PROVERBS 3:5-6

The journey you're traveling may be uncharted territory, but God knows the winding roads and crooked paths. Trust Him. He sees the path you're on. You may not see Him, but you'll look back and recognize His leading. Trust Him with your life. Those crooked paths... He promises to make them straight.

Journey to Purpose
31 Days of Faith Declarations

Thoughts   Prayers   Meditations   Declarations   Actions

_____

_____

_____

_____

_____

_____

_____

_____

_____

_____

_____

_____

_____

_____

_____

_____

_____

_____

ay 2

GOD HAS A PURPOSE

DECLARE - Before He formed me in my mother's womb, God knew me. So today, I'll not try to decide what I'll do with my life. Instead, I'll pray for revelation as to who I am and for what I am purposed.

Jeremiah 1:5

Don't waist your life with unfulfilling tasks. That desire... that vision... that dream... may be the purpose for your existence. Seek God now for revelation and move with determination toward your destiny. God has a purpose for your life and you were born to fulfill it!

Thoughts   Prayers   Meditations   Declarations   Actions

_____

_____

_____

_____

_____

_____

_____

_____

_____

_____

_____

_____

_____

_____

_____

_____

_____

ay 3

EYES HAVE NOT SEEN

DECLARE - Eyes have not seen, ears have not heard, neither has it entered into the heart of man the magnitude of what God has prepared for me.

1 Corinthians 2:9

God promises to do great things for those who love Him. He can intervene in the events of human history and cause people to perform His will on your behalf. There's no need for a daily horoscope or psychic hotline because eyes have not seen, ears have not heard and no man has conceived what God has prepared for you!

Thoughts   Prayers   Meditations   Declarations   Actions

_____

_____

_____

_____

_____

_____

_____

_____

_____

_____

_____

_____

_____

_____

_____

_____

_____

_____

Day 4

GREAT & MIGHTY THINGS

DECLARE - I will call unto you God. You will answer me and tell me great and unsearchable things. Things I do not know. Things fenced in and hidden. Things I cannot distinguish or recognize. Things of which I have no knowledge or understanding. I will call unto you God. You will answer me and show me great and mighty things.

Jeremiah 33:3

How do you know your purpose? Call unto God. He will answer you and show you the great and mighty things He has destined for your life.

Journey to Purpose
31 Days of Faith Declarations

Thoughts   Prayers   Meditations   Declarations   Actions

_____

_____

_____

_____

_____

_____

_____

_____

_____

_____

_____

_____

_____

_____

_____

_____

ay 5

GUARD YOUR HEART

DECLARE - I will guard my heart with all diligence. For out of it flow the issues of my life.

Proverbs 4:23

Your heart is the center of your intellect, emotions and will. It is where you pray, meditate, plan, decide, desire, think, love, grieve, receive, submit, ponder, doubt and believe. It affects everything you do. It is the source of true life and the center of your being. Above everything you protect, guard your heart with all vigilance, for it is the place from which your life flows.

Journey to Purpose
31 Days of Faith Declarations

Thoughts Prayers Meditations Declarations Actions

_____

_____

_____

_____

_____

_____

_____

_____

_____

_____

_____

_____

_____

_____

_____

_____

_____

ay 6

NO WORKS/NO FAITH

DECLARE - Faith, if it has not works, is dead, destitute of power, inoperative and ineffective!

James 2:17-18

Faith is more than just believing. Belief is simply acceptance of the facts as truth. Faith, however, is acting on that truth. Faith has arms and legs. Faith works! How hard are you willing to work toward your dreams, goals and aspirations? Your answer tells you how much faith you have in whether or not you will reach your God-given potential.

Journey to Purpose
31 Days of Faith Declarations

Thoughts   Prayers   Meditations   Declarations   Actions

_____

_____

_____

_____

_____

_____

_____

_____

_____

_____

_____

_____

_____

_____

_____

_____

DO THE WORK

DECLARE - I will be strong and courageous. I will do the work God has called me to do. I will not be afraid or discouraged, for my God is with me! He will not fail or forsake me.

1 Chronicles 28:20

When the Holy Spirit prompts, move with all diligence to complete the work He puts before you. He knows the time and the season. Don't delay. Get up now! Do the work! Don't be discouraged with the task. The Holy Spirit will empower you to finish it. He is right there with you.

Journey to Purpose
31 Days of Faith Declarations

Thoughts   Prayers   Meditations   Declarations   Actions

_____

_____

_____

_____

_____

_____

_____

_____

_____

_____

_____

_____

_____

_____

_____

_____

_____

_____

GOD IS FAITHFUL

DECLARE - For God is not unjust nor is He unrighteous as to forget or overlook my work and labor of love which I have shown toward His name and toward His people.

Hebrews 6:10

Your work may seem to go unnoticed and may not come with gratitude or accolades from others, but remember... God is faithful! He is just! He is righteous! He will remember the love you have shown Him as you have helped and continue to help His people. He will remember and reward your good works!

Journey to Purpose
31 Days of Faith Declarations

Thoughts   Prayers   Meditations   Declarations   Actions

_____

_____

_____

_____

_____

_____

_____

_____

_____

_____

_____

_____

_____

_____

_____

_____

Day 9

BE ANXIOUS FOR NOTHING

DECLARE - I will be anxious for nothing. In everything, by prayer and supplication with thanksgiving, I will make my requests known unto God. And His peace, which surpasses all understanding, will guard my heart and mind.

Philippians 4:6-7

Anxiety causes you to move too fast, taking you out of position to receive God's blessings. Don't be anxious. Everything will arrive in due season. Continue to pray and praise God. Allow Him to overpower all of your anxiety. He will give you peace that not even you can understand!

Journey to Purpose
31 Days of Faith Declarations

Thoughts   Prayers   Meditations   Declarations   Actions

_____

_____

_____

_____

_____

_____

_____

_____

_____

_____

_____

_____

_____

_____

_____

_____

_____

_____

Day 10

RISE LIKE AN EAGLE

DECLARE - I will wait upon you God. As I grow faint, You will renew my strength and power. I will rise like an eagle. I will run and not grow weary. I will walk and not faint. I will wait upon you God. You will renew my strength!

Isaiah 40:28-31

Do you not know? Have you not heard? The Everlasting God, the Lord, the Creator of the ends of the earth, does not become tired or weary. He gives strength to the weary and to him who lacks might, He increases power. Ask Him now for the strength and power to rise like an eagle, higher... even higher, above everything that would hold you down.

Journey to Purpose
31 Days of Faith Declarations

Thoughts   Prayers   Meditations   Declarations   Actions

_____

_____

_____

_____

_____

_____

_____

_____

_____

_____

_____

_____

_____

_____

_____

_____

_____

ay 11

CAST DOWN IMAGINATIONS

DECLARE - I will not allow negative thoughts to overtake me. I cast down imaginations and every high thing that exalts itself against the knowledge of God and I bring into captivity every thought to the obedience of Him.

2 Corinthians 10:5

Here is the first battleground - your mind! You're saying, "I don't have the education." "It's too late." "I tried that already." "I don't know enough." "I'm a failure." "I don't have enough money." "I can't try again." Stop it! Stop it now! God has given you the power to control your thoughts. Do not allow negative thoughts to overtake you. Cast down every condemning thought you are imagining. Everything that contradicts your vision, your promise, your purpose and your destiny... capture it and force it to submit to the Word of God. What does the Word of God say about you? It says you can do all things through Him who infuses inner strength into you, making you self-sufficient and able to do any and everything. Now... imagine that!

Journey to Purpose
31 Days of Faith Declarations

Thoughts   Prayers   Meditations   Declarations   Actions

_____

_____

_____

_____

_____

_____

_____

_____

_____

_____

_____

_____

_____

_____

_____

_____

_____

_____

RESIST & ENDURE

DECLARE - This temptation that entices me to sin is not beyond my resistance. God will not allow me to be tempted and tried above what I'm able to bear. He has provided me a way of escape and the power to endure.

1 Corinthians 10:13

Sin is a major decoy. Don't allow temptation to get you off track. You can resist! It may seem like it's too hard, but no temptation is above human resistance. God is faithful to His Word. He will not let you be tempted and tried beyond your ability, strength of resistance and power to endure. God has given you an escape route. Find it. Reach deep inside. God has given you the power to resist and endure!

Journey to Purpose
31 Days of Faith Declarations

Thoughts   Prayers   Meditations   Declarations   Actions

_____

_____

_____

_____

_____

_____

_____

_____

_____

_____

_____

_____

_____

_____

_____

_____

Day 13

BE OBEDIENT

DECLARE - I will obey you God. For I know that obedience from the heart is far better than any outward form of worship, service or sacrifice.

1 Samuel 15:22

There are some things on this faith journey that you'll have to give up. Whatever God is asking you for, give it to Him. Don't prolong this season and don't offer Him a sacrifice. It doesn't matter what else you give God if it's not what He's asking you for. You may be able to keep what you're trying to offer up. Don't sacrifice. Be obedient!

Journey to Purpose
31 Days of Faith Declarations

Thoughts   Prayers   Meditations   Declarations   Actions

_____

_____

_____

_____

_____

_____

_____

_____

_____

_____

_____

_____

_____

_____

_____

_____

_____

_____

ay 14

LAY ASIDE THE WEIGHT

DECLARE - I will lay aside the weight and sin that so easily beset me and I'll run the race marked out for me with patience and perseverance.

Hebrews 12:1

So today - strip off, throw aside, put away - anything that clings, anything that entangles, anything that burdens and anything that hinders you from running your race. You can't run if you're weighed down. Lay the heavy stuff aside, take your mark and don't stop running until you reach the finished line.

Thoughts   Prayers   Meditations   Declarations   Actions

_____

_____

_____

_____

_____

_____

_____

_____

_____

_____

_____

_____

_____

_____

_____

_____

 **ay 15**

NOW UNTO HIM

DECLARE - Now unto Him who is able to keep me from falling...

Jude 1:24

Only God is able to keep you from falling into sin, temptation, depression, loneliness, heartbreak, disappointment, discouragement and discontentment. Only He can keep you standing upright. Only He can give you wings to soar like an eagle. You can't keep yourself. Only God can. He is able. Let Him do it. In your darkest moment, with everything you have within you, find the strength to say 'Now unto Him who is able to keep me from falling'. He will not only keep you from stumbling, but He will allow you to stand in the presence of His glory blameless, without fault and with great joy.

Journey to Purpose
31 Days of Faith Declarations

Thoughts   Prayers   Meditations   Declarations   Actions

_____

_____

_____

_____

_____

_____

_____

_____

_____

_____

_____

_____

_____

_____

_____

_____

_____

ay 16

CONSIDER THE JOY

DECLARE - In my journey to purpose, I will not grow weary and lose heart. I will be joyous! I will fix my eyes on Jesus, the author and perfecter of my faith, who for the joy set before Him, endured the cross, scorned its shame and sat down at the right hand of the throne of God.

Hebrews 12:2-3

What will help you endure? The joy that is set before you! Consider the exhilaration of knowing you will fulfill your purpose and complete the work God has called you to do. Christ is our perfect example. It was for the joy of fulfilling what He came to this earth to do, that He endured such grievous opposition and bore His cross. Fulfilling your destiny should not be a burden. Consider the joy set before you (What is it?), lest you grow weary and faint in your mind.

Journey to Purpose
31 Days of Faith Declarations

Thoughts   Prayers   Meditations   Declarations   Actions

_____

_____

_____

_____

_____

_____

_____

_____

_____

_____

_____

_____

_____

_____

_____

_____

 ay 17

BE PATIENT

DECLARE - For I have need of patience. So that after I have done the will of God, I might receive what He has promised.

Hebrews 10:36

You have prayed, trusted, worked, waited, resisted, obeyed, believed and now... persevere, endure, be steadfast and be patient. The promise of God will surely come.

Journey to Purpose
31 Days of Faith Declarations

Thoughts Prayers Meditations Declarations Actions

_____

_____

_____

_____

_____

_____

_____

_____

_____

_____

_____

_____

_____

_____

_____

_____

ay 18

HE'S GREATER IN YOU

DECLARE - I am of God and belong to Him. I have defeated and over-
come all evil of the world, including satan, sin, trials, temptations, sorrow
and persecution because the Holy Spirit who lives in me is greater than he
who is in the world.

1 John 4:4

Don't think you're coming through without a battle. But guess what?
You've already won! For the God in you is far more powerful than the god
of this world. He who is in you... is greater!

Journey to Purpose
31 Days of Faith Declarations

Thoughts   Prayers   Meditations   Declarations   Actions

_____

_____

_____

_____

_____

_____

_____

_____

_____

_____

_____

_____

_____

_____

_____

_____

_____

_____

Day 19

NOT BY MIGHT

DECLARE - Neither by might nor by power, but only by God's Spirit will I be empowered to accomplish God's will for my life.

Zechariah 4:6

Military might, political power nor human strength can accomplish the work of God in our lives. We will only be fulfilled through the power of the Holy Spirit. Allow Him to empower you.

Journey to Purpose
31 Days of Faith Declarations

Thoughts   Prayers   Meditations   Declarations   Actions

_____

_____

_____

_____

_____

_____

_____

_____

_____

_____

_____

_____

_____

_____

_____

_____

_____

_____

Day 20

DRESS FOR BATTLE

DECLARE - I will be strong in the Lord and the power of His might. I put on the full armor of God so that I can stand against the strategies, schemes and deceits of the devil. I stand firm with the belt of truth, the breastplate of righteousness, the gospel shoes of peace, the shield of faith, the helmet of salvation and the sword of the spirit, which is the Word of God.

Ephesians 6:10-18

Now that you're dressed, stay alert and pray intensely in the Spirit always!

Journey to Purpose
31 Days of Faith Declarations

Thoughts   Prayers   Meditations   Declarations   Actions

Day 21

TRIUMPH OVER OPPOSITION

DECLARE - No weapon formed against me shall prosper. God has given me the power to condemn every tongue that rises against me in judgment. I am triumphant! Triumph over opposition is my heritage from God.

Isaiah 54:17

So, why fear your adversaries? Condemn them and triumph. It's your heritage!

Journey to Purpose
31 Days of Faith Declarations

Thoughts   Prayers   Meditations   Declarations   Actions

_____

_____

_____

_____

_____

_____

_____

_____

_____

_____

_____

_____

_____

_____

_____

_____

 **ay 22**

LIFE OR DEATH

DECLARE - I have the power to speak life into any situation I may face. I must be careful what I say because life and death are in the power of my tongue

Proverbs 18:21

Don't allow negative speech to kill your hopes and dreams. Speak life! It's in the power of your words.

Journey to Purpose
31 Days of Faith Declarations

Thoughts   Prayers   Meditations   Declarations   Actions

_____

_____

_____

_____

_____

_____

_____

_____

_____

_____

_____

_____

_____

_____

_____

_____

_____

_____

ay 23

HAVE DEFINITE AIM

DECLARE - I will run my race to receive the prize. I will not run with uncertainty. I have definite aim. I will not fight as one beating the air and striking without an adversary. Like a boxer, I'll buffet my body. Bringing it under subjection, handling it roughly, disciplining it with hardships and subduing it for the prize of the high calling!

1 Corinthians 9:24-27

Don't despise the rigid training necessary to run the race of life. Get in shape physically, mentally and spiritually. Know who your opponent is and take definite aim.

Thoughts   Prayers   Meditations   Declarations   Actions

_____

_____

_____

_____

_____

_____

_____

_____

_____

_____

_____

_____

_____

_____

_____

_____

_____

_____

 Day 24

BE THOU REMOVED

DECLARE - I will not pray for strength to climb my mountains. I will say unto these mountains, in faith, not doubting and never wavering, "Be thou removed." And it shall be done! All these things, whatever I ask in prayer, believing... I will receive.

Matthew 21:21

Here's the goal - mountain-moving faith! Whatever your mountain, JUST BELIEVE! It will be cast into the sea.

Journey to Purpose
31 Days of Faith Declarations

Thoughts   Prayers   Meditations   Declarations   Actions

_____

_____

_____

_____

_____

_____

_____

_____

_____

_____

_____

_____

_____

_____

_____

_____

_____

_____

Day 25

SACRIFICES OF PRAISE

DECLARE - God is my light and my salvation. Whom shall I fear? God is the strength of my life. Of whom shall I be afraid? In times of trouble, God will hide me in His secret place. My head will be lifted above my enemies and I will offer sacrifices of praise.

Psalms 27:1-6

Praising God in times of trouble is indeed a sacrifice. But in this sacrifice, God promises to hide you in His secret place. When He hides you, your enemies will not be able to find you. You will have a new perspective as your head is lifted above them. You'll be able to see over and above your problems. So in times of trouble, rejoice and offer sacrifices of praise. Victory is yours!

Journey to Purpose
31 Days of Faith Declarations

Thoughts   Prayers   Meditations   Declarations   Actions

_____

_____

_____

_____

_____

_____

_____

_____

_____

_____

_____

_____

_____

_____

_____

_____

_____

 ay 26

FROM SUFFERING TO GLORY

DECLARE - For I consider that the sufferings of this present time are not worthy to be compared to the glory that shall be revealed in me.

Romans 8:18

Can you even perceive that? The pain, hurt, resentment, and betrayal... all the sufferings you feel today can't compare, and are not worthy to be compared, to the glory God will reveal in you! This suffering will end. Receive it by faith and hold on! God wants to take you from suffering to glory.

Journey to Purpose
31 Days of Faith Declarations

Thoughts   Prayers   Meditations   Declarations   Actions

_____

_____

_____

_____

_____

_____

_____

_____

_____

_____

_____

_____

_____

_____

_____

_____

ay 27

NOTHING IS TOO HARD

DECLARE - You are the Lord my God. Nothing is too hard for You!

Jeremiah 32:27

God is answering your doubts with a question. "I am the Lord; God of all flesh. Is there anything too hard for me?" Resoundingly declare your answer. You are the Lord my God. NO! There is NOTHING too difficult for You!

Journey to Purpose
31 Days of Faith Declarations

Thoughts   Prayers   Meditations   Declarations   Actions

_____

_____

_____

_____

_____

_____

_____

_____

_____

_____

_____

_____

_____

_____

_____

_____

_____

Day 28

GOD WILL DELIVER

DECLARE - I will not bring to the moment of birth and not cause delivery says God. Nor will I who cause to bring forth shut up the womb.

Isaiah 66:7-9

I know it looks like the promises of God will never come to pass, but before you travailed, you brought forth. Before your pain came, you delivered. It's already done! Don't let anxiety and impatience abort the promise. God will cause delivery!

Journey to Purpose
31 Days of Faith Declarations

Thoughts   Prayers   Meditations   Declarations   Actions

_____

_____

_____

_____

_____

_____

_____

_____

_____

_____

_____

_____

_____

_____

_____

_____

_____

_____

_____

ay 29

YOU CAN'T IMAGINE

DECLARE - Now unto Him Who is able to do exceedingly, abundantly, far over and above all that I dare imagine, pray, desire, ask, think, hope or dream.

Ephesians 3:20-21

You thought you saw the vision. But God is able to do exceedingly above and far beyond what you could have ever envisioned or dreamed of. You can't imagine what God can do for you! To God be glory forever and ever. Amen!

Journey to Purpose
31 Days of Faith Declarations

Thoughts   Prayers   Meditations   Declarations   Actions

_____

_____

_____

_____

_____

_____

_____

_____

_____

_____

_____

_____

_____

_____

_____

_____

_____

ay 30

REMEMBER GOD

DECLARE - I will not say in my heart that the power and might of my hands have brought me to this place of promise. But I will earnestly remember the Lord my God, for it is He who gives me the power to prosper.

Deuteronomy 8:17-18

God has delivered! Did you ever doubt? Oh ye of little faith. Now don't let your blessings cause you to be haughty. Remember God. For it is He alone who gives you the power to fulfill your purpose.

Journey to Purpose
31 Days of Faith Declarations

Thoughts   Prayers   Meditations   Declarations   Actions

Day 31

POSSESS THE PROMISE

DECLARE - The Lord my God has placed the promise before me. I must move forward and take possession as He has commanded. I will not be afraid or discouraged for He has gone before me and His promises are now mine.

Deuteronomy 1:21

Just as the children of Israel were commanded to take possession of the land God promised them, when God gives you a promise of your future, you must move forward and take possession. Don't be afraid or dismayed. Possess your promise. Now!

Journey to Purpose
31 Days of Faith Declarations

Thoughts   Prayers   Meditations   Declarations   Actions

EPILOGUE

I hesitated in writing this book in fear of giving the erroneous impression that I have arrived at my purpose. I have only arrived at the revelation that this journey to purpose is not a destination at which you arrive, but a continuous path. Only with this revelation did I truly come to peace with the never-ending cycles and fully understand what it means to be content and joyous in every season of my life. But having walked such a short distance on this journey, I have yet to learn the lessons of those who have allowed time to give them wisdom only it can impart. But there is an urgency to write of my short journey. The urgency is personal, but I know that I am not alone in this necessity to fulfill purpose.

I have come to realize that fulfilling purpose is a choice. God has given us the power to choose our lives. That choice began with Adam and Eve. God had a perfect plan, but He did not force Adam and Eve to be obedient to His plan. He gave them a choice; the same choice we have today. We should look to Christ as our perfect example of obedience and acceptance of the will of God for our lives. Christ also had a choice and He chose to bear His cross, laying down his life to fulfill the purpose for which He was sent to this world. Christ had the greatest purpose ever, but He said we would do even greater things.

You too are here for a great purpose. I believe God is birthing and delivering visions all over the world that will directly affect the world as we know it today and worlds to come. Therein lies the urgency. There is no time for wasted lives, wasted years, wasted weeks, wasted days or even wasted moments. The time for us to realize our purpose and move forward... is now!

If not now, when? I have asked myself this question many times as the unknown answer permeated the air. As I wrote the 31st Declaration, *Possess the Promise* from Deuteronomy 1:19-21, the answer resonated ever so clearly. If not now, maybe never! It seemed so harsh, so final. I thought surely God is merciful and will give us all the time we need to fulfill what He put us on this earth to do. But I have seen physical death come to those whose dreams were still inside of them, having lost all hope of becoming what they should have been. Still, surely God gives second and third and fourth chances. But when I put the book of Deuteronomy in historical perspective, I found that God is indeed a God of unlimited chances, but He is also a God of judgment.

In Deuteronomy Chapter 1, Moses told the children

of Israel why they had wandered in and around a place called Kadesh Barnea for 40 years…

> "It takes eleven days to go from Horeb to Kadesh Barnea by the Mount Seir road.) In the fortieth year, on the first day of the eleventh month, Moses proclaimed to the Israelites all that the LORD had commanded him concerning them;" (1:2-3).

The journey from Horeb to Kadesh Barnea should have only taken 11 days. But, it was 40 years after they departed on the journey that Moses began to tell the children of Israel their history…

> "East of the Jordan in the territory of Moab, Moses began to expound this law, saying: The LORD our God said to us at Horeb, "You have stayed long enough at this mountain. Break camp and advance into the hill country of the Amorites; go to all the neighboring peoples in the Arabah, in the mountains, in the western foothills, in the Negev and along the coast, to the land of the Canaanites and to Lebanon, as far as the great river, the Euphrates. See, I have given you this land. Go in and take possession

of the land that the LORD swore he would give to your fathers—to Abraham, Isaac and Jacob—and to their descendants after them." (1:5-8).

Moses continued in verse 19.

"Then, as the LORD our God commanded us, we set out from Horeb and went toward the hill country of the Amorites through all that vast and dreadful desert that you have seen, and so we reached Kadesh Barnea." (1:19).

It was 11 days into their journey when they came to the place where they would cross over to possess the land promised to them. They were at Kadesh Barnea, their gateway to destiny. Moses continued to relay their history…

"Then I said to you, "You have reached the hill country of the Amorites, which the LORD our God is giving us. See, the LORD your God has given you the land. Go up and take possession of it as the LORD, the God of your fathers, told you. Do not be afraid; do not be discouraged." (1:20-21).

The Lord had brought the children of Israel to the precipice of their promise – Kadesh Barnea. They should have chosen to move forward and possess the promise. This should have been the end of the journey, but it wasn't. Despite the Lord's command and pleas from Moses to *fear not nor be discouraged*, the children of Israel needed more confirmation that they could indeed do what the Lord told them they could do; win the battle and possess the land. Moses continued to share their history…

> **"And ye came near unto me every one of you, and said, We will send men before us, and they shall search us out the land, and bring us word again by what way we must go up, and into what cities we shall come. And the saying pleased me well: and I took twelve men of you, one of a tribe: And they turned and went up into the mountain, and came unto the valley of Eshcol, and searched it out. And they took of the fruit of the land in their hands, and brought it down unto us, and brought us word again, and said, It is a good land which the LORD our God doth give us." (1:22-25).**

But, the good report of two of their spies did not convince the children of Israel to move forward. Even after tasting the good fruit of the promised land, they listened to the naysayers and disobeyed the Lord's command to possess the land. Moses continued in Verse 26...

> **"But you were unwilling to go up; you rebelled against the command of the LORD your God. You grumbled in your tents and said, "The LORD hates us; so he brought us out of Egypt to deliver us into the hands of the Amorites to destroy us. Where can we go? Our brothers have made us lose heart. They say, 'The people are stronger and taller than we are; the cities are large, with walls up to the sky. We even saw the Anakites there." (1:26-28).**

Without avail, Moses continued to plea...

> **"Then I said to you, "Do not be terrified; do not be afraid of them. The LORD your God, who is going before you, will fight for you, as he did for you in Egypt, before your very eyes, and in the desert. There you saw how the LORD your God carried you, as a father carries his son, all the way you went until you reached this place." In spite of this, you did not trust in the LORD your God, who**

went ahead of you on your journey, in fire by night and in a cloud by day, to search out places for you to camp and to show you the way you should go." (1:29-33).

Their unbelief and disobedience brought God's judgment. Moses continued...

"When the LORD heard what you said, he was angry and solemnly swore: "Not a man of this evil generation shall see the good land I swore to give your forefathers, except Caleb son of Jephunneh. He will see it, and I will give him and his descendants the land he set his feet on, because he followed the LORD wholeheartedly." Because of you the LORD became angry with me also and said, "You shall not enter it, either. But your assistant, Joshua son of Nun, will enter it. Encourage him, because he will lead Israel to inherit it. And the little ones that you said would be taken captive, your children who do not yet know good from bad—they will enter the land. I will give it to them and they will take possession of it. But as for you, turn around and set out toward the desert along the route to the Red Sea."

(1:34-40).

Although the children of Israel repented and decided to move forward to possess the promised land, it was too late. God's judgment was final! The gateway to destiny had been closed. The Lord had withdrawn His provisions and protection. Moses continued to tell the Children of Israel their history...

> "Then you replied, "We have sinned against the LORD. We will go up and fight, as the LORD our God commanded us." So every one of you put on his weapons, thinking it easy to go up into the hill country. But the LORD said to me, "Tell them, 'Do not go up and fight, because I will not be with you. You will be defeated by your enemies.' "So I told you, but you would not listen. You rebelled against the LORD's command and in your arrogance you marched up into the hill country. The Amorites who lived in those hills came out against you; they chased you like a swarm of bees and beat you down from Seir all the way to Hormah. You came back and wept before the LORD, but he paid no attention to your weeping and turned a deaf ear to you. And so you stayed in Kadesh many days—all the time

you spent there." (1:41-46).

The children of Israel were never meant to spend 40 years of aimless wandering around Kadesh Barnea. It was their holy gateway to destiny. But they refused, out of fear, doubt and unbelief, to possess the promise - and God judged them to die in the wilderness, at Kadesh Barnea.

Are you at your Kadesh Barnea? Are you at the precipice of your promise? Are you at your holy gateway to destiny? If so, don't reside there. It's a gateway not a dwelling place. Go on through. Receive the Words of the Lord as told to the children of Israel. *"You have dwelt long enough in this place. Turn and take your journey."*

The Lord has set the promise before you. Go in and possess it. Do not fear nor be discouraged. Do not hesitate. The Lord your God has gone before you and will fight for you. You have seen the Lord come through for you many times on this journey. He has carried you as one would carry a son. He has been with you every step of the way, until you came to this place. This is Kadesh Barnea, your place of destiny or judgment. Don't rebel. Do not fear. Do not doubt. Only have faith and possess your promise!"

Journey to Purpose
31 Days of Faith Declarations

Thoughts   Prayers   Meditations   Declarations   Actions

_____

_____

_____

_____

_____

_____

_____

_____

_____

_____

_____

_____

_____

_____

_____

_____

_____

_____

Thoughts	Prayers	Meditations	Declarations	Actions

Thoughts   Prayers   Meditations   Declarations   Actions

_____

_____

_____

_____

_____

_____

_____

_____

_____

_____

_____

_____

_____

_____

_____

Thoughts   Prayers   Meditations   Declarations   Actions

_____

_____

_____

_____

_____

_____

_____

_____

_____

_____

_____

_____

_____

_____

_____

_____

_____

_____

Journey to Purpose
31 Days of Faith Declarations

Thoughts   Prayers   Meditations   Declarations   Actions

_____

_____

_____

_____

_____

_____

_____

_____

_____

_____

_____

_____

_____

_____

_____

_____

Thoughts   Prayers   Meditations   Declarations   Actions

_____

_____

_____

_____

_____

_____

_____

_____

_____

_____

_____

_____

_____

_____

_____

_____

Journey to Purpose
31 Days of Faith Declarations

Thoughts   Prayers   Meditations   Declarations   Actions

Thoughts	Prayers	Meditations	Declarations	Actions

Journey to Purpose
31 Days of Faith Declarations

Thoughts   Prayers   Meditations   Declarations   Actions

_____

_____

_____

_____

_____

_____

_____

_____

_____

_____

_____

_____

_____

_____

_____

_____

_____

Thoughts   Prayers   Meditations   Declarations   Actions

Journey to Purpose
31 Days of Faith Declarations

Thoughts   Prayers   Meditations   Declarations   Actions

_____

_____

_____

_____

_____

_____

_____

_____

_____

_____

_____

_____

_____

_____

_____

_____

_____

Thoughts   Prayers   Meditations   Declarations   Actions

_____

_____

_____

_____

_____

_____

_____

_____

_____

_____

_____

_____

_____

_____

_____

_____

_____

_____

Journey to Purpose
31 Days of Faith Declarations

Thoughts   Prayers   Meditations   Declarations   Actions

_____

_____

_____

_____

_____

_____

_____

_____

_____

_____

_____

_____

_____

_____

_____

_____

_____

Thoughts   Prayers   Meditations   Declarations   Actions

_____

_____

_____

_____

_____

_____

_____

_____

_____

_____

_____

_____

_____

_____

_____

_____

ACKNOWLEDGEMENTS

I WILL BLESS THE Lord and remember all of His benefits. He forgives my iniquities. He heals my diseases. He redeems my life from death and destruction. He crowns me with loving-kindness and tender mercies. And He satisfies my every desire with good things. I acknowledge and give honor to my earthly guide, the Holy Spirit, my heavenly intercessor, Jesus Christ and the creator of my life, Almighty God.

To my mother, Essie Bradford, thank you for realizing that my journey does not lead me down a familiar path. It is a journey of faith and many times I am blinded to the dangers and pitfalls you may anticipate before me. Thank you for doing what only a nurturing mother can do. Thank you for your weighty intercessory prayers.

To my sisters, Melvina LaFlore, S'cie Ward, Wanda Adams and Kaye Rand, I thank you all for allowing me to learn from your lessons and benefit from your blessings. It is because you came before me, that I can move with such determination.

To my friend Kim, who talked so much about her

Lord that I was moved with godly envy. I would listen intently and say to myself, "*Who is this Man?*" Thanks Kim. Now I know!

To my friends, Charrisse Coates, Roger Robinson, Theman Taylor and Rossie Turner, thank you all for faithfully walking with, supporting and encouraging me.

Thank you Marie Trotter, my editor and the most talented and creative writer I've ever known. Some years ago when I asked you to edit a spiritual article, you said you weren't comfortable speaking for God. Now, when asked to edit this book, there was no hesitation. I thank God for anointing your talent, giving you an ear to hear what the Spirit of the Lord is saying and imparting in you the Godly wisdom and deep revelation to be comfortable as a gatekeeper of His Word.

To the spiritual leaders and worshippers whose messages and music continue to strengthen my faith, I say thank you. Although I know you only by the Spirit, your ministries have been so profound in my life that I must thank you by name. Thank you Yolanda Adams, All Together Separate, Mark Chirona, Creflo Dollar, Kirk Franklin, Fred Hammond, T.D. Jakes, Crystal Lewis, Donnie McClurkin, Nicole C. Mullen, Myles Munroe, Gary Oliver, Chris Rice, Marvin Sapp, Trin-i-tee 5:7 and CeCe Winans.

To the men of God who have pastored me on this journey, thank you. Pastor Johnny Lawrence, thank you for my firm foundation. Bishop Steven Arnold, my first faith teacher, thank you for speaking faith directly into my spirit and birthing the vision God has given me for my life. Pastor Horace Hockett, thank you for instilling in me the fear of the Lord while teaching me the importance of holiness and obedience. Bishop Kenneth Dupree, the Lord sent me to you for delivery. Thank you for helping me push.

I also acknowledge Elder Michael Steven Moore. Thank you that every time you saw my faith faltering with statements of defeat, at the mercy of lifeless words, you would ask one simple question, *"Have you sent out today's Faith Declaration?"* I thought I needed more, but you knew that all I needed was to hear the Lord speak faith through me. Thank you for ministering a personal word to me on a daily basis.

To Diann Mustin, I asked God for clarity on the epilogue to this book, He sent you, His word made flesh. I thank Him and you for the manifested revelation of Kadesh Barnea.

And finally, I thank God for those who came across my path and didn't see the vision. You provoked me to press deeper into the Lord for truth and clarity. To God be the glory forever and ever. Amen.

Journey to Purpose In 31 Days e-Seminar

The Journey to Purpose In 31 Days e-Seminar is an intensive 31-day study and application of the 31 Faith Declarations found in this book. In 31 days, you will learn how to start your journey to purpose. If you know what your purpose is, you'll learn how to maintain the strength to keep pressing. And if you're at the precipice of your promise, you'll learn how to cross over. In these 31 Days, you'll receive the faith you need to continue your journey to purpose. Register online at JourneytoPurpose.com.

Robinson Omnimedia Publishing & Studios' books may be purchased for educational, business or sales promotional use. For information about special discounts for bulk purchases, contact:
Robinson Omnimedia Publishing & Studios
Books@RobinsonOmnimedia.com
888-904-9993

To arrange for Deborah Robinson to speak, contact:
RobinsonOmnimedia.com
Media@RobinsonOmnimedia.com

Made in the USA
Middletown, DE
18 July 2021